Silk Road To Africa

for

JetSet Global Publishing, LLC

BIO

OF

GLENN T. SMITH

WORLD TRAVELER, MUSICIAN AND AUTHOR OF

"SILK ROAD TO AFRICA"

ALSO

PRESIDENT AND FOUNDER

OF

THE AFRO~ASIAN CONNECTION

Born in San Francisco, Calif.

Traveled to Japan early in life, where the Afro~Asian
journey began.

Silk Road To Africa

The Afro Asian Connection

How China will move Africa and its'
Descendents into the 21st Century

Glenn T. Smith

To order additional copies of this book, contact:
Xlibris Corporation
1-888-795-4274
www.Xlibris.com
Orders@Xlibris.com
83933

Contents

Acknowledgements

For

Silk Road to Africa

First and foremost I want to thank my mother,
Lee G. Henderson, for her unwavering love.

Second to my father, Henry L. Smith,
for his strength and courage.

I want to say to my sister, Linda F. Smith,
Thank You for being more like dad, Love Ya!

To my brothers, Anthony and Dewayne Smith,
you guys are awesome.

To all the members of SF Tradewinds.
What a journey we had together.

To Linda Kral, for all of your mentoring.

To Raul Yanez, Thanks for looking at the first draft,
and consulting with me.

To God, for giving me the vision,
because without a vision a people will perish.

Thank You

Glenn T. Smith

Introduction

THIS JOURNEY HAS taken nearly 20 years to complete. All the pieces are in place for this book to reveal and introduce what's been written in the stone for thousands of years. That is the relationship between China and Africa and how China in particular with its emergence as a super power, will assist Africans and its descendents into the 21st century.

What this book will show the readers is the devastation that has and is still taking place in the Sub-Saharan region of Africa. The book will also show the tremendous growth in the Asia, fueled by manufacturing, high-tech, computers, entertainment, travel and higher education, which equals too the largest growing middle class in the world.

Forty years ago, there was hardly any difference between the living standards in Asia and Africa. Both emerged from a verity of colonial experiences. By 1996, Asia has moved ahead faster than Africa in the Sub-Saharan region. There are four main factors that account for the rapid development of the East Asian region and its attainment of a developed economy: 1). Education – producing an educated labor force and growing middle class capable of absorbing technology and investments from abroad; 2). The development of agriculture; 3). The adoption of economic policies and 4). Political stability.

Africa's economic situation and its overall living standards have declined according to my research which I will give more detail as the book unfolds. In a period of world advancement, Africa has not succeeded in keeping pace. National Geographic has documented and photograph, starting as far back as 1980's, the relative decline and its current crisis. Africa's people lack an ample supply of safe drinking water, and over half of the population has no ready access to health services.

Beijing '08, a new superpower steps up. China. I'm so excited about the future of Africa and equally so about the 2008 Summer Olympics in China

The Olympics will showcase China as never before. Over the past three decades China has prepared its' people for this moment in history.

The construction of Olympic Park is monumental. The technology necessary to construct such a project and man power are all the things needed for Africa's infrastructure. Dam's for irrigation, housing for shelter, hospitals, roads, electricity. It's the breakthrough needed, and China is ready to provide the resources.

The long history of both Africa and China are clearly documented. What's not, for most people, is the vision of the future of China and Africa together. Silk Road 2 Africa will pull the veil back so all can see and understand the tremendous alliance that's happening and that was foreseen by the author 20 years ago. The writing's on the wall, (The Great Wall of China that is). For centuries this message has been waiting to be deciphered. The Silk Road 2 Africa has done that and more. We will travel together back, then to future. On this amazing journey we'll learn about inventions that contributed to slavery, how war sustained nations and commerce, and the trade of slaves brought Africa to its knees and built other nations prosperity.

This book time has come. It is necessary to finally let the world know how important it is to bridge the gap between the two. Because of the socio, economic and historical theme, it will pique interest from educators, government representatives; both local and state; business owners, the growing numbers of Afro Asian interracial relationships and Generation X. Due to the emergence of Hip Hop in fashion and sports; all over the globe and especially in Asia, the cultures are coming together. In Japan, Korea, Vietnam and the Philippines, they are listening, watching and imitating Black Americans.

Chapter 1

Get-N-the Booty

That's the Way of the World

WEBSTER'S DEFINITION OF Booty – 1. Plunder taken from an enemy in wartime. 2. Stolen or seized goods. 3. A valuable prize, award, or gain.

Since the fifth century BC, till the end of the Ming dynasty, more than 2,000 years of Chinese military strategy has helped build one of the greatest nations on the planet. From Alexander the Great, Napoleon, Caesar, Cleopatra to General Patten, all used military strategies to get the booty, keep the booty then use the booty to get more booty.

Ancient China and Japan have a rich historical background in military warfare, which is one of the reasons why China and Japan have reached the level of success in the world today.

Back in the 70's during the Vietnam War, a singing group call the Temptations, has a protest song call "War". The lyrics, "War, what is it good for, absolutely nothing, say it again", has stayed with me since then. War has made the world what it is today. From the 80's, another group Earth, Wind, and Fire said it so well, "That's the Way of the World", and in the 90's Teddy Reily of the group Black Street, "It's a Booty Call". The Africans were taken from their land, or I should say stolen and seized, as the most valuable prize.

This chapter will give a better view of the world today; it will look who got the booty and also look at who was the booty.

A nation is born out of military involvement, from the first tribes to large communities. A nation cannot become unified into an empire unless individual tribes or states are unified under one flag, one goal or one purpose. Technological achievements and government stability are paramount if the nation is to continue its future. Look at Kenya today, the fighting and disruption. Also, look at the black community across the United States and you see a community fallen apart at the seams.

As a result of my interest in slavery and the reasons for it, I decided to research with the hopes of providing answers to the dilemma that Africans and its decedents were facing in the early 80's and still are today, 2008. I knew that war, military development and the invention of weapons played an important part in the development of the slave trade. The Europeans merchants, and their military provided the means for the religion to take hold of the country they invaded and the trade of human beings became to norm for Africa. Hugh Thomas' book, "The Slave Trade", provides excellent references and a great historical account of the slave trade. The book shows evidence that the countries with the military weaponry were able to force Africans in slavery. In the next chapter I will focus on the military strength of these nations and will show that the lack of any military advancement in Africa was a contributing factor for slavery to flourish in this region.

Chapter 2

Nation Building

MILITARY DEVELOPMENT IN Europe was a natural state of affairs. From Aristotle, his rang true, "Humanity is divided into two: The Masters and the Slaves." The Europeans always felt they were and are the masters of the game of life. The Catholics, Christians, and Muslims all developed warfare as a means of furthering their nations. Military science allowed prolonged conflict between nations, states and people from other regions. Shield and helmets, bows and arrows, slings, chariots, the use of the horse and the invention of the gun made warfare the dominate force of conquests and the means to spread religion, create commerce and get the BOOTY.

The Roman Empire rules by Caesar conquered and enslaved large numbers of people. He then insisted that they worship him and his likeness. Alexander the Great conquered Egypt and most of Northern Africa. Below the Sub-Saharan region military development had not developed as the Europeans, Japanese, and China. This is one of the reason this region, when the Europeans came to Africa, they were able to come in and take the booty. As a consequence, nowhere in the history of mankind was such a cruel and methodical system put in place to enslave a group of people other than what Hitler did to the Jewish people. Without a unified nation its people will perish.

That is why I look toward the East. The Chinese did not participate in the destruction of the African continent. When the Spaniards and the Portuguese came to Japan and China, they found a unified nation with a strong military and a leader with a populace ready to defend the nation.

The Quest for a Democratic System

Wars, tyrannical regimes, insurrection and widespread corruption are indicators that a country's economy will decline, poverty will worsen, domestic industry will stagnate and international investment will be withdrawn. Democracy grows at a speed which differs from country to country. There is not a standard pattern or blueprint for societies which differ fundamentally from the west.

The principles associated with democracy, however, are universal. These principals include good government, an independent judiciary, and observance of human rights, a free press and leadership competition through elections. The need to nurture a democratic culture and practices cannot be overemphasized. A democratic form of government cannot guarantee economic growth and prosperity for all.

One of the dangers for the democratic process in Africa would be the impatience of the populace. At present, no regional network of political parties operates in Africa. Such a network would be desirable, allowing like-minded parties to interact and exchange experiences.

This would contribute to a strengthening of the democratic spirit, deepen understanding and generate solidarity. At a national level, a government might find it easy to intimidate or destroy a small democratic party, but as part of a wider African network, a democratic party could receive protection or at a minimum, public attention beyond the national borders.

What I would like to do now, is talk a little about the Black Liberation movement in the United States of America during the 1960's. For those of you who may be too young to remember, The Black Panthers, where at the forefront of this movement. What the movement failed to understand is how a nation is born. A nation is born out of war and conquest of itself. Unifying its people, which can only occur through a tremendous loss of life, is how China, Japan, England, France, Spain, the Arab Emirates of Northern Africa and the United States of America were formed. Africa, below the Sub-Saharan, on the other hand, did not participate in nation building during this period of the 12th, 13th, and 14th century. There are a host of reasons, which I will go into more deeply, for now lets' explore navigation.

Navigation was the science that brought the world closer together, the way all invention does throughout history, for the betterment of mankind. Shipbuilding, which grew out of many years of architectural brilliance that catapulted China onto the world stage as far back as the 12th century, is another area that Africa below the Sub-Saharan area did not participate. Because of this, the exchange of knowledge did not take place enough for this region the flurious. Based on my research these are the things that prohibited growth of this region in the areas of math, science, and warfare.

Chapter 3

Why the Sub-Saharan is losing the Global Race

AFRICA BELOW THE Sub-Sahara region is in dire need of a viable infrastructure, including the establishment of credible administrative, legal and financial institutions. Economic development will not take place without investments in science, technology, which cannot flourish, without first commenting to the development of the human researches. Yet, Africa is confronted by a qualitative decline in its education system, placing it far below the international mainstream.

The need to develop management and administrative skills in Africa is apparent. Africa is losing its market share in international trade. One of the solutions is for a revitalization of the agriculture. 70% of the 500 million people in sub-Saharan Africa depend on the agriculture for a living. Yet, agricultural output per head is barely growing. It is crazy that Africa cannot feed itself now and must import foodstuffs to the detriment of the economy. There is not healthy economic future for most African countries if they remain organized as they are now. Without redrawing boundaries, there could be a pooling of resources into zones of regional cooperation. Africa will not play a world role nor garner a larger share of the international economic action, unless it can form more effective states.

The population has grown at an explosive rate of 3.1% caused by a step fall in the mortality rate a continuously high fertility rate, approximately 6.5

children to every woman, much the same thirty years ago and twice as high as in South Asia at present. This population surge has been a major factor in impeding the rate of social and economic advancement.

The present extent of HIV and AIDS incidence in Africa is shocking. Sixty to seventy percent of all HIV-positive and AIDS cases worldwide occur in Sub-Saharan Africa. Adding to the human devastation, there will be ten million orphans. Roughly half the bed capacities in many of the hospital in Africa are already taken up by AIDS patients, according to Greg Behrman, author of "The Invisible People". There will be ten million orphans left without a net the catch them to provide food, shelter, and a family structure for growth and development. Unless the problem is addressed; financial resources, human resources, and political attention are bound to go to waste.

Most of Sub-Sahara Africa, although some hope is forming on the fringes, has turned into a battleground of contending dooms: AIDS, overpopulation, poverty, starvation, illiteracy, corruption, social breakdown, vanishing resources, overcrowded cities, drought, war and the homelessness of war's refugees. For decades, Africa could count of the cold car as an economic resource. The U.S. and the former Soviet Union elbowed each other through African proxies, pouring in money to prop up pro-Western or pro-Communist surrogates. Now the big powers' priorities have gone elsewhere. 400 years ago Africa's inner rhythms of development were shattered by the invasion of the Europeans, who brought in alien controls, boundaries and new forms of government. This is what has driven me to write this book, the belief that because of China's non involvement in the slave trade, because of the tremendous ability for China to invent, organize, and govern. It (China) will have a huge impact on Sub-Saharan Africa. Jung once wrote, "Different people inhabit different centuries. This is China's century, and Africa's turning point in history. When the colonialists pulled out, they left the economic, political and cultural infrastructure reconfigured in such a way they the new countries served Europe better than they served one another. What is often missing is a social contract between the governing and the governed. In fact, millions of Africans have found that their economic energy, their sanity and even their survival depend of how they succeed in outmaneuvering the state.

Chapter 4

The Moses Syndrome – How Religion played a role in Slavery

"Humanity is divided into two: the masters and the slaves."

Aristotle, Politics

LET US FIRST examine together what I mean by the Moses Syndrome. The Bible has played a tremendous role in the conditioning and salvation of African slaves. It is the driving force for a clear understanding of today's problems in the United States as it relates to African Americans and our relationship with God and the hereafter. Growing up in a household that was headed by a Catholic father, Baptist mother, and an Aunt how was a Jehovah Witness gave me a tremendous view point about the influence religion played in our household, and community.

Two things quickly come to mind. 1. Rev. Ike, a charismatic minister who traveled around the country preaching the gospel of success and hope. 2. The Rev. Jim Jones, who took hundreds of African Americans to South America and committed suicide. The reason I bring these two men up is to illustrate the power of the Bible and how people used its' teachings the keep people either in the right frame of mind or used the old and new testament too keep weak and use the power of hope to bring tragedy.

During the time of slavery in the United States, Christianity was the religion of the slave masters. The Old Testament with its reference to Israel being in captivity and Moses freeing the Jews from the Egyptians had a powerful impact on the thinking process of the slaves. The keepers of the slaves found that converting slaves the Christianity would civilize them and keep them under control. The use of this story encouraged the slaves to have faith in the teachings of the Bible, which meant having faith in God, who would deliver them from captivity. Deliverance from the clutches of the evil masters has been the hope of millions of people displaced from their true homeland from hundreds of years.

In the early seventeenth century, it became customary for slaves in Africa to be baptized before their departure from Africa. Most slaves had not previous indication that there was such a thing as a Christian God. This requirement was first laid down by King Philip the third of Spain in 1607. Upon arrival into the new world, slaves were branded and beaten into submission. Unlike the nations that engaged in the slave trade, the Africans that were traded did not have a religion that unified its people. Islam and Christianity over the centuries through the crusade established itself and its people as rulers of those less fortunate.

The Catholic Church, one of the most powerful institutions on the planet, engaged in the transport of slaves, as did the Protestants, Presbyterians, and Islam all engaged in the transport of slaves in the name of their religion. The nations that these religions are attached, engaged through warfare, building not only their nations, but also establishing and protecting trade and commerce. Get-N-the Booty, that's the way of the world, has been and will always be.

As the years went by, the dependence on the church grew as a place for gathering together, after long hours in the fields, and Sunday's was a time for hope, salvation and planning escapes.

And escape is what a lot of slaves tried to do. We must remember that the slaves that where brought on that long voyage and made it to either Brazil, Cuba, West Indies, and the United States, had to be very strong in mind and body, and a human being, with the love of family, and connection to the community of villages that made up life. So yes, being brought to a place not of there doing, they wanted to escape. Most of these attempts where done under the guise of the church.

The magnificent book "The Slave Trade", by Mr. Hugh Thomas, gives such an insight into the world of slave trade, especially how Islam, Christianity,

Chapter 5

Enter the Dragon
Masters of the Game

CHINA'S HISTORY IS marked with secrecy, myth and legend.

One thing is for sure China did not enslave Africans during the Diaspora. Let's look at how China was able to fend off the Europeans during the 14th and 15th centuries and why China with its' vast military and Navy did not engage in Slavery.

Research for this chapter open my eyes to the tremendous history of China's inventions in the areas of navigation, astrology, gun powder, writing, and military stratagems.

The history of China's military is a blue print for success today in our corporate environment. Go to any bookstore and peruse through the business section, you will find several books on winning in business from the perspective of China or Japan's success.

Policies and Strategies are the main principals that brought China through the most amazing accomplishments in the world.

Survive and then conquering, Chinese nobles had to have the components of administrative and organizational strength that even today could rule and run large corporations. From The Seven Military Classics of Ancient China, by Ralph D. Sawyer an International Consultant, has open the door on the tremendous volumes of writings about China's emergent as a super power even before the establishment of the new world order. The five critical talents Kings, Generals or Nobles must process are courage, wisdom, benevolence, trustworthiness, and loyalty.

These are the traits that as we move into the 21st century China, Korea, Taiwan, Hong Kong, Viet Nam, Japan and India will start to revive ties forged in cultural revolutions that's taken place through the world. As we progress throughout this journey I'll address how the Afro-American struggle has ignited this Cultural Revolution and is now ready to reap some of the benefits, including Africa.

When the first East Asian traders came to Africa in the year 1418 (*Asia, INC. 1995), in the bazaars of the kingdom of Malindi (in present-day Kenya) Chinese traded their porcelains and silks for East Africa's gemstones, woolens and carpets. The question is how did the Chinese get there? That we will talk about later.

Trade flowed between Africa and Asia between 1988 and 1992, doubled from $8.1 billion to $16.7 billion. That outlook is projected now to amount to $480 billion by the year 2025. Not surprisingly, Asian trade delegations are elbowing each other out of the way to ensure they get a big slice of the business. To put things in perspective perhaps things could have been so different. 50 years ago Asian and African leaders met in Bandung, Indonesia, to chart a common way forward, instead the African leader forge an alliance with Russia, the rest is history.

Let's take a deeper look at Sub-Saharan Africa, mainly South Africa. From outcast, after Apartheid, is on track to become the locomotive of Sub-Saharan Africa, according to sources such as Time Magazine, and Asia, Inc. When in 1994 Nelson Mandela won the election in the country's first multiracial election marked the final chapter in South Africa's economic, cultural and sporting isolation. Since then, more than 25 Asian countries have reportedly begun looking for consular representation in Pretoria, then the administrative capital. Businesspeople from Thailand, Malaysia, Indonesia and China have been quick to respond to the challenge. It started in 1995, when Malaysian property company Landmarks Bhd. Announced it was planning to take a 27 percent state in South Africa's Boland Bank Ltd., in a complex deal worth $75 million.

At the time according to the then international trade and industry minister, Rafidah Aziz, South Africa will become the "staging point" for Malaysian companies seeking to enter the southern African region. South Africa needs all the overseas help it can get in rebuilding an economy severely weakened by the 1980's withdrawal of multinational corporations anxious not to be accused of propping up the apartheid regime. According to Louw Burger, then managing director of ABS Asia (a subsidiary of Amalgamated Banks of South Africa).

Now, what I'm about to share with you is going to be something of a surprise to a lot of people, even most Chinese themselves. "Genetic evidence does not support an independent origin of Homo sapiens in China." This statement is from Scientists in the Chinese Human Genome Diversity Project. I bring this up to an even deeper connection that is being revealed through genetic findings that traces Chinese origins to Africa. From the Science section of the SF Chronicle, dated September 1998, I was overjoyed to see this article. It confirmed and validated the Afro Asian Connection on an even deeper level. The article stated that most of modern China's population, one fifth of all people living today, owes its genetic origins to Africa, an international scientific team reports in research that undercuts the claim that modern humans may have originated independently in China.

Published in the then Proceedings of the National Academy of Sciences, the study is the product of the Chinese Human Genome diversity Project, a consortium of seven major research groups in the People's Republic of China and the Human Genetics Center at the University of Texas at Houston.

Li Jin, the senior scientist guiding the genetic analysis, said the study is based on analysis of the gene patterns from 43 different ethnic groups in China and Asia. Jin said the findings may disappoint some of his fellow geneticists in China, where recent fossil discoveries that attest to the great antiquity of human settlement in East Asia have been a source of national pride.

From these findings, in my humbled opinion, is why it is so befitting that through the growth of China's people, and all the accomplishments that have taken place over the last 2500 years, that China now has an opportunity to bring these developments to the Sub-Saharan area of Africa.

Chapter 6

Lost in Space without a Place The Rise and Fall of the African American Community

Endangered Family

DURING THE 1950'S, 60's and the 70's, the African American Community was striving, growing and thriving. Fathers and mothers were in abundance. Even though racism, segregation, was still everywhere, the community as a whole was still moving forward. Kids had community activities such as the Boy's and Girl's Club, was a place where adults cared and supervised young children and children had respect for one another. All across the United States, and deep in the south college attendance where high and high schools was in full effect. Newsweek reported on the Endangered Black Family in the 90's, in 2000 we are in the midst of a crisis. The current report titled "Black in America", reported by Soledad O'Brian, showed the tremendous problems facing Black America today.

For many African-Americans, marriage and childbearing do not go together. After decades of denial and blame, a new candor is emerging as blacks struggle to save their families. In the 50's when a young lady got pregnant they were considered unique. In the 70's, no one was ostracized, though it still wasn't something "nice" girls did. 90's, it was regarded as "normal." Now it's common place. "And there doesn't seem to be anything happening to reverse it." Let's take a look at some statistics. For blacks, the institution of marriage has been devastated in the last generation: 2 out of 3 first births to black women under 35 are now out of wedlock. In 1960, the number was 2 out of 5. And it's not likely to improve any time soon. A black child born today has only a 1 in 5 chance of growing up without two parents until the age of 16, according to University of Wisconsin demographer Larry L. Bumpass. 30 years ago, one quarter of black families were headed by women. Today the situation has only has only grown worse. A majority of black families with children are now headed by one parent. It was not always so. Before 1950, black and white marriage patterns looked remarkably similar. In 1990, Census figures shows, 65 percent of children of black single mothers were poor, compared with only 18 percent of children of black married couples. Statistics tell only part of the story. Equally important are the intangibles of belonging to an intact family. "Growing up in a married family is where you learn the value of the commitments you make to each other, rather than seeing broken promises," says Roderick Harrison, chief of the Census Bureau's race division.

Fatherless homes boost crime rates, lower educational attainment and add dramatically to the welfare rolls. Among the poor, a staggering 65 percent of never-married black women have children, double the number for whites. The result is what John Hopkins University sociologist Andrew Cherlin calls "an almost complete separation of marriage and childbearing among African American." Young boys in particular need male role models. Without a father, who will help them define what it means to be a man? Fathers do things for their children that mothers often don't. Though there are obviously exceptions. More and more, black men aren't there to build marriages or to stick around through the hard years of parenting. The question we're too afraid to confront is, why. I look to a field of medicine that is often overlooked in the black community, which is Psychiatry. As a community, the toll, psychologically that has shaped our community has really never been looked that until now with the book "Come on People" by Bill Cosby and Alvin F. Poussaint, M.D., this book opened up a dialogue that until now has not been taken seriously by the black community. My research to the effect that slavery has had on the African American, how the lost of love ones from the civil rights wars effected the physic, how being victimized by racial injustices play a huge role in the lost of self esteem for the African American community. "Living the Truth", by Keith Ablow, M.D., shows how to transform your life through the power of insight and honesty. It takes a great man and women to look within themselves and face the truth. This leads us up to the "D" word, Depression. It would take another book on this subject alone, what I'm doing is opening up further the path Mr. Cosby, and Dr. Poussaint, started. Another book that unlocks the mystery and myths of depression, which I know will take us from the darkest depths of our souls is "Unstuck". As Dr. Gordon says, "Depression is the defining disorder of our time." Some of the conditions that are recognizable are feelings of deep sadness, hopelessness, and worthlessness, irritability, withdrawal and suicidal despair. Some out of the box thinking towards a cure combines a variety of kinds of psychological guidance and instruction which includes: Exercise, meditation, guided imagery, self-expression through words, drawings, and movement, yoga, nutrition and supplements, acupuncture and herbal therapies, and a variety of spiritual practices such as Buddhism.

The code of the street:

Why is the code of the street so important to the Black Community? Is it a sense of pride that drives our young and women to such degrees as robbery, drug dealings and consumption? Homicide is the leading cause of death for the Black males. Wow, that's staggering to think that the psychological damage to our race has come to this. Let's look at one city in California. Oakland from 1992 through 2007 homicide rate was out of control. I challenge you to share this information with your sons and daughters, friends and family members. In 1992 the total was 175, in 1993 the total was 167, and in 1994 the total was 151, the total in 1995 was 153, in 1996 the total was 102, in 1997, 110, in 1998 the total was 81, and in 1999, 68, the total in 2000 was 85, in 2001, 87, in 2002 113, in 2003, 114, in 2004, 88, in 2005 94, in 2006, 122, in 2007, 135. A grand total of 1,602, and all unsolved.

That's just in one city, not to mention from that same time period across the United States what kind of lost of lives we are talking about. We do not know how many future Miles Devises we have lost. Future people like James Brown, Angela Davis, and Martin Luther King. We just don't know, we do know that a great number of young black men and gone. Families torn apart, communities stripe of brain trust. Do you not know that this is a huge cause of depression? Well, it is. As I struggled with my own feelings of worthlessness, and self esteem, I sought to find a cure. After traveling to Japan, I started to understand that you can change. I learned about Kaizen, which means "continuous improvement." I saw the Japanese, who endured tremendous devastation after the bombing of Hiroshima, and Nagasaki, to rise out the ashes and become a super power. I think it's important to look towards the east as and means of unlocking secrets that could solve problems within the Black community. Especially China with its long history of achievement, invention, military feat, and its people hold the key for Africans and its descendants to strive in the 21st century.

Behavior change doesn't have to be difficult.

Although most therapists probably would agree that behavior change usually is difficult and does not happen overnight, that does not have to be the case. In 1985 Morty Lefkoe, the founder of the Lefkoe Institute developed the first in a series of interventions (The Lefkoe Method) of which I participated, that actually do produce rapid and lasting change. I first heard about The Lefkoe Method after reading Re-Create Your Life. This introduced me to a powerful method and encourages me to seek Mr. Lefkoe for further in depth consultation. Most people attribute their problems to their circumstances. In fact, our undesirable behavior and feelings are largely the result of our beliefs, not things outside of us. Mr. Lefkoe says, "When you eliminate negative beliefs, such as, I do not deserve, relationships don't work, life is difficult; you literally change your life."

These are the concepts that I believe will change how we are a culture most look at how to solve these tremendous problems facing the black culture here in the United States.

January 1, 2007 came to an end for Denver Broncos starting cornerback Darrent Williams, 24, was fatally shot in a drive-by while in a rented limousine. February 2007, just two months into the year, Baltimore police has logged 45 homicides. Three masked assailants confronted Vic Fenner, 17 and shoot him in the head. Mr. Fenner became the 46th just within 2 months of 2007. No motive and not one suspect. In San Francisco, December 31, 2006, shooting in the Bayview leaves 3 dead, a total of 85 slain, black of black, and not one suspect or arrest.

Do you remember the Million Man March? I do, it was a historical event. Can you imagine all those men in jail? Will that's what we have. 1.2 million Black men are in jail as of this writing. More young black males are in prison than in college, homicide is the leading cause of death for black males between the ages of fifteen and thirty-four. Nearly 51 percent of all African American families are headed by single women. Although African

American makeup 12 percent of the population, we account for more than 35 percent of all AIDS cases. December 2007, as Christmas trees and family gather, there's another end-of-the-year ritual in Oakland, a candlelight vigil for the murdered. Violence is so woven into the culture that murder has become a symbol of manhood.

In major cities across the nation, children are dying form gun violence at alarming rates. Each year, more than half o the victims of gun homicides are African-Americans. Last year in Chicago alone, 24 public school students were shot to death. So far this school year 2008, the number has already reached 20. Most of the violence occurs in Black neighborhoods like Englewood of the South Side of Chicago.

I grew up in a time that was marked with violence. That violence was perpetrated by KKK, CIA, FBI, and local police. During the 1960's, Martin Luther King, Malcolm X, and scores of African Americans were killed trying to bring change to America. 1970's was a time of renewal, James Brown, I'm Black and I'm Proud, Black Panthers believe we should protect our own community, by any means necessary. Angela Davis, H. Rap Brown, and Stockley Carmichael, gave us power in the spoken word. Music, art, fashion furished all across the black community. A black renaissance emerged, the struggle was on high. The Black Muslims gave us the entrepreneurial spirit. Ownership of businesses was the code of Black Muslims, which is how you are able to control your own destiny. The 1980's was a period of time that forces started pulling apart the Black Community.

Immigration: Its affect on African Americans

A new wave of immigration is changing the complexion of the American landscape. Immigrant from Latin America and Asia represent the fastest growing domestic markets. While Asians and Hispanics were only a few drops in the national melting pot just 30 years ago, the now account for nearly 15% of the American population. You don't need a crystal ball to catch a glimpse of the New America. Hispanics and their off springs will make the black population wake up one morning and not know what happen, and that time is upon us now. In New York City, Hispanics are about to become the largest minority group, surpassing blacks. While in cities such as Miami, San Antonio, and El Paso, they already constitute an absolute majority of the population. These new demographic trends represent just the latest chapter in what sociologist Nathan Glazer calls the "permanently unfinished story" of America, a nation that continues to take in more immigrants each year than all the rest of the countries of the world combined. Immigration has always been the source of the remarkable self renewing power of the American economy. Similarly, it has always been a source of social unrest and political discord.

The Black community with its high rate of murders, which is ripping out a large segment of the community, deaths from AIDS, 1.2 million men in jail, 54% of Black households headed by a women, and NO IMMIGRATION. You can see the crisis in Black America that most civic leaders are not addressing. That is Africans do not come to the United State to be called African Americans. Now, I don't think you need too much conversation around the question of immigration and how it affects the African American community. If these issues are not addressed in an out of the box thinking, one that includes Asia, the community will be in deep trouble. Thus the title of this chapter, "Lost in Space without a Place." San Francisco, where I was born and raised, has long been the capital of Asian America. During the past 20 years Asians have more than replaced the whites who fled the city for surrounding suburbs. The San Francisco Chinese are no longer the poor immigrant of the popular imagination, washing dishes in small Chinese restaurants or stitching garments in a stuffy sweatshop, living in crowded flats on the quaint but squalid streets of Chinatown. Today they constitute a prosperous consumer market; with 41% owning their own homes, starting businesses and helping others do the same that come from mainland China.

As long as a nation of people does not have a vision on how we are going to remedy this problem, we have to look at other means of solving this problem.

What is Africa to Me?

> *Copper sun or scarlet sea, jungle star or jungle track, strong bronzed men, or regal black women from whose loins I sprang when the birds of Eden sang? One three centuries removed from the scenes his father loved, Spicy grove, cinnamon tree, What is Africa to Me?*
>
> By Countee Cullen, Heritage.

From the time since we as African Americans were taken from the shores of West Africa, the questions of, What is Africa to Me?, Why did they do this to us? Am I an African, or am I an American.

Every Black American who thinks about or journeys to Africa seeks an answer to that question. After reading, watching movies about the slave trade and researching in the bowels of several libraries, I came across a story about a correspondent from Time, who spent 2-1/2 years on the continent of Africa, by Jack E. White, in his own words. "I think of Africa as the motherland. On Goree Island, a rocky outcropping in the harbor of Dakar, Senegal, stands the Slave House, through which thousands of Africans where brought and sold. I wondered if some unknown ancestor of mine had walked through this very doorway and could not hold back the tears".

Africa and its lost children hence lost in space without a place.

Lacking detailed knowledge of precisely where our ancestors come from, whether they were Fon, Ashanti or Serer, African Americans have tried to adopt the continent as a whole as a placed of origin. But that indiscriminate embrace poses problems of its own. What, for example are African Americans raised in the Christian faith to make of religious and cultural traditions such as female circumcision, which is still widely practiced in Africa today? Our centuries in America have transformed black Americans into a Western people. Whether or not we rejoice in the fact, not many of us can ever go completely home again. From a psychological standpoint we have lost our emotional connection to our past. Yet from time to time black Americans have immersed themselves in the trapping of African culture. Many of us celebrate pseudo-African holidays like Kwanzaa, in addition to Christmas. We applaud these trends, because they stand in contrast to the shamed repudiation of Africa and everything African that dominated our thinking as recently as a generation ago.

A Change is Goanna come:

This has been a theme throughout the history of "Black America". Either from a messiah, social change like Brown vs. The Broad of Education, changes in voting rights, you name it we as a people, a community, a queasy nation have been waiting for change. If you look all around changes are coming at lightning speed except in the "Black Community".

You can see how immigration is changing the makeup of what once use to be a majority black community, is now truly a multi-racial community. Technology is changing how we learn, communicate, travel, and eat. Every aspect of our lives is being impacted by technology, except in the "Black Communities" across the United States.

The "Black Community" is in the ashes of a deep depression. The community as a whole is simply unhappy, anxious, or confused. You may not agree with everything I'm about to say on this subject, all I ask is that you the reader keep a open mind and let's discuss and take this journey together of exploration that I know will lead to understanding and change.

As I sought to answer questions I discovered a wealth of information regarding change. The majority comes from "Corporate America". As I fought to change and improve myself I became exposed to what is called "change agents".

We have the power to change anything. It's been done countless times. For example, John F. Kennedy changed the United States, with just a few words, Martin Luther King, changed people's hearts, with his words and his actions. Gandhi changed India and influenced and changed the world.

We as ordinary people can accomplish extraordinary things. We change and influence our families and our communities my modeling these change agents. How you may be asking? Let me explain. The idea that inner change makes outer change possible has always been part of spiritual and psychological teachings. It's an idea that hasn't been addressed in the "Black Community" loud enough. This is the paradigm shift that's needed in our families, communities and within us. As change agents we can show individuals how to go through personal change so they can alter how they see the world. From author Robert E. Quinn's book "Change the World", I discovered a model that can be used as a guide in transforming not only our lives, also our communities.

Another concept that I've discovered during my research is a term called "groupthink"; it paralyzes our world and impedes innovation and progress. Based on the beliefs we hold and the choices we make, determine our destiny. Just look at the black community and you'll see the tragic effect that unhealthy thinking has on the lives, and families of our community.

When fear, power, and control dominate our communities' people descend into territorial behavior. The time has come to do something about it, but our community leaders are unclear as to how to proceed. I do not claim to have all the answers, but I do know I have an answer. Based on knowledge from Judith E. Glass, author of "Creating We", I discovered yet another change agent. I've believed for a long time that the answers to our community problems can be found in corporate America. In Judith E. Glass's book she illustrates how this can be done from a corporate level and then we can transfer that knowledge to our communities. In order for a business to strive and survive its people have to innovate and cooperate to solve problems and create change. A person cannot strive without growth. As Judith Glass says in her book, "Growth, the very essence of change and transformation, is about pushing back what is and making room for what can be. The dynamic tension between what is and what can be pervades the environments in which we work and live every day". I have searched for an answer to the problems that are bringing down our communities across America. By working for some of the most prestigious companies and having been coached by the best executive coaches around, I discovered how change makes companies grow, strive and create environments that are very productive and nourishing. We are at a point of change in the world, and here in the United States. Being transformational is about looking at our values, thoughts, and behaviors. We become transformational change agents through choice – our own.

> **"Nonviolent resistance does not seek to defeat or humiliate the opponent but to win his friendship and understanding. The aftermath of nonviolence is the creation of the beloved community, while the aftermath of violence is tragic bitterness".**
> **Martin Luther King, Jr.**

Violence in the black community has created the most destruction in the United States, the world has ever seen.

It's amazing how rich in creativity and innovation the Black Culture has been over the hundreds of years that we have been in the United States, in the areas of fashion, music, dance, sports, business, politics, civil rights, inventions, medicine and as time continues to march on the psychological wounds get deeper and deeper. With the great minds in our community, I ask why we as a people can't create solutions to the tremendous problems facing our people.

Chapter 7

Breakthrough to Possibility Rewriting our Story

Reconstructing Our Past

THE PATHWAY TO getting unstuck and dispensing long-held psychological stumbling blocks offers a profound opportunity to transform our cultural histories. We as a people have endured and because of this ability, the survival of the fittest, has allowed our race to flourish under tremendous odds. It is time now to leave behind the world of struggle and enter a vast universe of possibility. Leave circumstances that block us in our pursuit for happiness and achievement. These are based on assumptions, and beliefs we carry with us. Eradicating these assumptions and beliefs has been a lifelong pursuit. As a community we have not been able to keep up with the pace of change that is taking place in the world. We are now in the 21st century and our communities are still functioning on the out dated assumptions that perpetuates practices that are illogical our counterintuitive to understanding how the world is now operating. Our communities across the United States are in need of a total shift of perceptions, beliefs and thought processes. It is time to transform our entire world.

Using Asia as a model for transformation will be the next level of restructuring the Black Community. In Africa as in Asia, also here in the US, we are divided by culture, language, political ideology religious, philosophies and geography. Because of the challenges that faced Asia as well as Africa back in the 1940's and how Asia from 1945 to 1995, half a century, went from rags to riches through forging economic integration, technology, especially telecommunications, travel and increasing mobility of its people, has made a coherent region we can learn from.

Being preoccupied with its own survival, almost no one in the Black Community has the faintest idea that what is going on is Asia today will radically change the world. The economic resurgence of Asia, driven by an aggressive global network of Chinese entrepreneurs and off-shore money, is moving in the direction of dominance in the world. The modernization of Asia economically, politically and culturally is by far the most important event taking place in the world today. China, the Great Dragon, is flexing its economic and political power to influence not only the region, but the world. Especially in Africa, below the Sub-Saharan, will get the needed attention to grow, develop and finally come into the 21st century. China is not only central to the Pacific region, but also here in the Black Communities across America. The Chinese true force is a secretive sophisticated network, invisible to most. It is decentralized global and family and education oriented and most of all, fabulously rich. It is the phenomenon of the Overseas Chinese. There are 57 million of them and they have been around for centuries, but only now is the world becoming aware of their awesome presence.

The rebuilding of the Black Communities across the United States is going to happen with or without the help of its own people. The most important aspect of the Overseas Chinese is the less glamorous small and medium-size enterprises all across America. Look at all the local restaurants, cleaners, dentists, car dealerships, and a host of mom and pop shops like herbal and health businesses, not only in the predominantly Chinese districts but all across our communities. These are the types of models the Black Communities have to look at. The successes of these networks are driving change at a pace most African Americans are not keeping pace with.

The New Urban Middle Class:

A new middle class, the size of which the world has never before seen, is being created is Asia. In 2000 the Gallup Organization released the results of the first ever scientific national poll of China, the world's most populous country. Its conclusion: a billion Chinese want to become rich and buy millions of TVs, washing machines, refrigerators, I-phones and IPods. It comes as no surprise that 84 percent of Chinese households that already own a TV, the 23 percent that spent their hard-earned money on refrigerator or the 35 percent that purchased a washing machine in the last few years. Some 68 percent of the Chinese polled desired to "work hard and get rich." The rise of the middle class is revamping Asia's economic structure. Once dependent on exports for economic expansion, Asia can now also rely on domestic demand to fuel growth.

What is happening in China, as reflected in that Gallup poll, is happening throughout Asia. The average Asian's living standard is bursting out of "survival" into consumption. If Asian economies continue their 6 to 10 percent annual expansion rate of the last decade, their middle classes will double or triple in the next decade. The Asian middle class, not counting Japan, could number between 800 million and 1 billion people by 2010, resulting in a stunning $8 to $10 trillion in spending power. That's in the neighborhood of 50 percent more than today's U.S. economy. It took Britain's middle class nearly a century to evolve. In Asia today, that process is being accomplished in a little more than a decade.

Entertaining Asia:

Middle-class economic status opens the door to the big world of entertainment. Now we come full circle in understanding the concepts that this book has presented so far, and what the future holds for both the African American community and the Asian and Hispanics families moving into what was mainly 80 to 90 percent Black, which now stands at about 45 to 55 percent Black, has to come to grips with each other in ways no one saw 10 or 20 years ago. These communities all across America are becoming truly multiracial communities. In Asia, the family unit has long been the foundation of society. The family system, instead of the government, provides social, economic and emotional support to the individual as well as the family itself. Within these communities you'll see a greater economic integration, cultural exchange through the businesses that Asians set up and the values of education and success that is sorely lacking in large sectors of the Black Communities.

Based on a wonderful book titled, "Megatrends Asia", written by the world's leading trend forecaster, John Naisbitt, talks about how the United States has to look to the east as a guide post for the 21st Century, I bring it further into the Black Community, because the east in moving into these communities in large numbers which we will continue this journey of exploration and discovery.

The richness of Asian civilizations, its people, culture, religions and a long glorious past are now being brought into the African American communities all across America. And with that the Black Communities leaders are facing challenges that need immediate attention. We have to explore new ways to cooperate, to create opportunities in employment and investments for the less developed sectors, and to maintain competitiveness instead of anger towards each other.

The Way of the Future for Black America:

The diversity of Asia and the varying levels of wealth within, gives examples of new ways to explore business opportunities. For the first time a new paradigm is emerging. The experiment of the Afro Asian Connection has a profound implication to the future of America. By modeling Asia's "Golden Age of Growth", which has a success plan that has elevated its people and economies to create opportunities in technology, finance, manufacturing, aviation, automobile industry and investments, is the way of the future not just for its regions but as a model for the world, according to John Naisbitt's, analysis. After careful study, I have come to the conclusion that the Afro Asian Connection is vital to the survival of African Americans and its descendents for generations to come.

Africa and African American's infrastructure Challenge:

The Great Wall of China as an infrastructure project is one of the largest construction projects in history, snaking the length of one twentieth of the earth's circumference. Capital, technology, and management skills are the hallmark of China, Japan, Korea, Vietnam, Hong Kong, Indonesia and the Philippines. Let's take a look at some of the developments that have been done in this region.

China has put $6 billion in roads, a port and telecom links for Shanghais new Pudong district. Three billion into the 1,500 mile railway linking Beijing to Kowloon. Then there is the $20 billion hydroelectric dam at Three Gorges. Africa below the sub-Saharan is in dire need of this king of technology especially hydroelectric power.

South Korea invested $13.4 billion in a high-speed train link between Seoul and Pusan, and another $50 billion has been spent on thirty new power plants, including seven nuclear plants, and a new $5 billion airport.

Thailand Telecom Asia has built 2 million telephone lines costing $3 billion. Another $11 billion has gone into 3,800 megawatts of electricity projects since 1995. Thailand is also building a brand new airport costing $3.5 billion and the Siemens-built Bangkok Electric Train that cost $720 million.

Its mind boggling that Asia will spend $1 trillion as of the 21st century mainly on energy, telecommunications and transportation. One of the reasons for Asia's huge cash reserves is its high individual savings rate which is why they are able to engage in such a high level of advancement that we as Americans are only saving a fraction in comparison which is why our roads and schools are not funded. One of the issues that the Black Community has to deal with is drug use, commercial sex, high prison incarceration, and HIV/AIDS. With the low rate of all the above in Asia, especially Japan, gives more reason to look at the Afro Asian Connection to improve all the conditions that are pledging our communities all across the United States.

The Asia boom that's taking place will provide the United States one quarter or more of its total economic growth for years to come, according to an analysis by The Economist. Asia, which includes India, and the United States are the two places in the world that allow entrepreneurs free range to revitalize and build up the economies, and they are the two places that will truly prosper as we move deeper into the 21st Century.

The Long View – Savings and Investments equals Growth-

Asian countries have high savings rates, averaging around 30 percent. It is reported that urban Chinese have about $200 Billion outside the nation's banking system. Per capita income in China is $2,600. There are more than 80 million Chinese earning between $10,000 and $40,000 a year. We also know that there are more than a million millionaires in China. With the rise in consumer spending the saving rate will go down, and more investment capital will have to be raised outside the region. To channel savings into productive capital and let money make money for the Asians, tremendous opportunities are opening up in the field of personal finance. The region's major financial institutions are launching unit trusts and mutual funds to mobilize domestic savings and help its citizen's hedge against inflation.

Within the Black Community its leaders can learn how to model the Chinese when it comes to providing its communities with guidance. We as a people have to understand that we don't have all the answers. And when the community in mired in self-deception it's hard to see past being a victim in society, especially when you think that the society you live in, is the enemy. Besides China, the wealthy individuals in Singapore, Taiwan, Hong Kong and Malaysia offer great untapped potential.

Our communities cannot save it self-

By now, it should be beyond a doubt that for African Americans Asia is the site of a model that can be used to bring our communities and its people out of the destruction that has pledged our communities now for over 25 years. It will take our leaders from just talking about the problems facing our communities to taking action. It's going to take great skill and tenacity to study and model how especially the Chinese have built wealth. This can be accomplished by embracing the commitment of the power to change, and to become change agents and super influencers.

Today's new urban Asia is as sophisticated and in many ways just as exciting than Western cities. Urban Asian consumers are knowledgeable, modern and keen to embrace the global lifestyle. Nury Vitachi, who writes for the South China Post and the Far Eastern Economic Review, describes the Asian middle-class phenomenon: "Executives in Asia have become rich at warp speed by taking full control of their own lives. They invest a great deal of time in their work, they use stratagems, tactics for triumph and survival, to scramble up the corporate ladder, and they demand payment in cash, so that they can make their money work as hard as they do."

Signs of affluence are everywhere. Traveling around Asia, no matter how rich the Asians become, signs of their frugal nature are still apparent, and they are very cost-conscious. Most save the increases in their incomes, and many prefer to put those savings into fixed or other income-generating assets. Stocks, land and property are their favorites.

Many affluent Asians still regard financial security as the most important form of security, and they are confident that Asia is the place to be to achieve that. While many have begun to savor the good life, they are not letting go of their top priority of education for their children. Education is looked upon as the most important contributing factor to success in life.

Despite the rise in their assertiveness, Asians still look to the United States and not so much to Europe for ideas and trends. Hence the Afro Asian connection becomes apparent. The music, fashion and entertainment industries, including sports are one of Afro Americans strongest assets.

African Americans influence on Asia

Let's start with Russell Simons, creator of Phat Pharm clothing line. Urban fashion has two elements in it. One is the so called "street credibility", in other words the creative ability of Black people to create something out of nothing. The other is crime.

Russell Simons is the God Father of Hip Hop. Hip Hop is now the ambassador of fashion and music around the world. Russell Simons helped sell the culture of hip-hop by identifying, nurturing and promoting artists, rappers, comics, designers to create commercial products and a business that didn't exist a generation ago. There were no rap stars, no movies starring rappers of clothing lines bearing their names or, for that matter books written by people involved with them. Russell Simons built the business of hip-hop from the ground up to a multibillion-dollar industry. Hip-Hop has changed the world. It has taken something from nothing and made it global. It has become the creative touchstone for edgy, progressive and aggressive youth culture around the world especially in Asia.

Sean John, aka, Puff Daddy is renowned for his innovation in music and fashion, restaurant ownership and entertainment management of the biggest stars in the world. Notorious B.I.G., made history with his rivalry with Tupac Shakur. Also, Mr. Combs has recorded and produced several of the biggest names in the industry with the likes of New Edition, Method Man, Babyface, and Mariah Carey. Sean John started his career in the 1990's when he talked the head of Uptown Records, Andre Harrell into hiring him as an intern.

Master of the game of cool is Jay-Z. Following the footsteps of his mentors Jay-Z has also created an empire that has tremendous influence around the world, especially in Asia. Shawn Carter. As co-owner of Roc-A-Fella Records, Rocawear clothing, the 40/40 club and Armadale Vodka, makes Mr. Carter one on the leaders not only of Hip Hop but also of the Black Youth movement. He has just signed a major sneaker deal with Reebok and took and minority stake in the New Jersey Nets NBA franchise, which he plans to help relocate to his home borough of Brooklyn. Now the newly formed Carter Administration. In 2004, Jay Z, Damon Dash and third Roc-A-Fella principal, Kareem Burke, sold the remaining interest in the company to Def Jam for $10 million. In January, 2006 Mr. Carter accepted a position as president and CEO of Def Jam. Reporting to Universal Music brass Doug Morris and L.A. Reid, Jay Z got an office at 825 Eighth Avenue, sole control of Roc-A-Fella, which would remain its own entity, in its own name and perhaps most importantly, the right to the masters of the eight albums he released under Def Jam from 1997 to 2003. With this, he ushered in a new era.

R. Kelly, who has been instrumental in creating images in video's and music that, changed how we deliver music to the world. His music is edgy and pushes the envelope regarding social issues in our community. Producers like Rodney Jerkins, aka, Dark Child has been a tremendous influence on modern music today. Usher Raymond has built a dynasty in the music industry. He is the only R&B male artist to see 10 million units since Michael Jackson. This brings us to the Prince of Rock and the King of Pop. Michael Jackson and Prince, two of the most creative people in the Black Community and the music industry as a whole have created and produced some of the most electrifying moments in music history. Janet Jackson, Destiny's Child, Mya, Ciara and AfroAsian artist like Amerie, and Kristal K, are leading the way in music, fashion and business.

In the jazz arena, we have Miles Davis and tenor sax pioneer John Coltrane who invented "Cool and B-Bop, which grew into Hip Hop. One of the giants in the business industry is Berry Gordy, founder of Motown who brought to the world Diana Ross, Marvin Gaye, Michael Jackson, Smokey Robinson and Stevie Wonder and a host of talented people that change the face of music from then till now.

From politics, to civil rights the list starts with Dr. Martin Luther King, Jr., who gave his life for the rights of all Americans. His legacy is felt around the world. During the plight of Blacks in the United States, South Africa was also going through its struggle, which brought about Nelson Mandela. Now in the 21st century, we have BARACK OBAMA, president of the United States of America. We all know his story, and what a remarkable story it is. One of the things history will write will be his upbringing, which was an Asian background wither than a Black background. In other words President Obama is not a product of the Black experience; he is like Tiger Woods, a product of the Asian experience.

The sports world is full of names that have influence the world, especially Asia. With the likes of Michael Jordan, Carl Lewis and now the top sports figure and Afro Asian, Tiger Woods.

The new Millennium will continue to bring about tremendous change and the Black Community is again on the fore front of that change in areas

Entertainment, fashion, music, business, hair & beauty, arts and crafts. In the areas of technology, and science is where we can forge an alliance with China and India. These two giants, in this century will truly change how we live and do business for the foreseeable future. Now is the time to look to the east before we lose sight of what's most important, which is the survival of our communities. Our children future depends on the decisions we make now.

In the areas that I have been talking about so far, it's very clear that the future for the west will be the east. For Africans and its dependence it's even more important to focus on Asia. ASEAN, the Association of South East Asian Nations, whose member are Indonesia, Thailand, the Philippines, Malaysia, Singapore and Brunei, encompasses a population of 359 million people and an import market of $226 billion.

Two places to find solutions to the problems of Black America and Africa I believe are Hong Kong and Singapore. Both successfully evolved out of poverty and decay to become models of urban planning and control. In the 1950s, Hong Kong was a huge shantytown populated by Chinese seeking refuge from the communists. In 1953 fire consumed the homes of 50,000 people and urban planners had to figure out how to house these people as well as the hundreds of thousands of Chinese who kept pouring into the city.

Forty years later urban planners flock to Hong Kong to study how the colony works. Hong Kong residents have housing, more than half the populations' lives in modern public housing developments and business has ample office space. Fortune magazine named Hong Kong the world's "best city for business."

Singapore arguably is the world's most modern city, if measured by its telecommunications infrastructure, and definitely one of the most conservative, if measured by its paternalistic social policies. The "Singapore Model," as summarized by Asiaweek has 10 policies that Singapore officials see as the key elements of its success. In "Megatrends Asia" by John Naisbitt whose book I've drawn most of my stats are as follows:

1. Strong Government; 2. Long Term Planning; 3. Local and Foreign Investment; 4. Clean Administration; 5. Education for all; 6. No Welfarism-Home Ownership; 7. Family Values; 8. Law & Order; 9. Communal Harmony; 10. Nationhood.

Urban Migration:

Urban migration rolls on and development continues. Urbanization is wide-ranging, because the modernization of Asia, economically, politically and culturally is by far the most important event taking place in the world today. Asia's young population is in its consumer-spending prime. Hong Kong, Singapore, Taiwan and South Korea, has more than 65 percent of its population between fifteen and sixty-five years of age. Asia's middle classes are changing the economic, social and political landscape of the region. They are better educated, marrying, but having few children. The young urban middle class of Asia is sophisticated, internet savvy and are very competitive.

The new middle class represents tremendous purchasing power, which will result in tremendous political power. Mike Ferrier, the Hong Kong based regional director of U.S. advertising giant McCann-Erickson, says, "It shows that Asia has turned from a production market into a consumption market. Asia used to only manufacture goods for the West. Now the west is sending things here."

Dawn of a New Day: India Inc.

In 1996 John Naisbitt, author of Megatrends and Megatrends Asia, predicted that Indian, Inc. would be a nominate force in Asia, and the world. In 2006, on the front cover of Time magazine, the lead article is "India Inc., Why the world's biggest democracy is the next great economic superpower."

India awakens, fueled by high-octane growth; it is the land of opportunity. India faces a host of social problems. But with a middle class that is 300 million strong, the nation is poised to challenge China as Asia's colossus. This is great for Africa, because now you have two giants that will need the natural resources and the human resources that are in such dire need of nurturing and development. So as India grows so does the impact that it can have on Africa. Here's why. India's GOP topped $800 billion in 2005.

Education is one the highest priorities in India. For that reason Indians like Pradeep Singh spent ten years in the United States at Texas Instruments and Microsoft to get educated. After returning to Bangalore, he launched NetQuest (India) Private, which sells electronic services and software products. G. Jagannath Raju earned a Ph.D. from the Massachusetts Institute of Technology and started Systematics Inc., a Lexington, Massachusetts based robotics company. Government incentives lured him back home after twenty years. He plans to build robots for India's nuclear power plants, mining industry and aircraft manufacturers.

Bombay's Boom:

If you want to catch a glimpse of the new India, with all its dizzying promise and turbocharged ambition, then head to BOMBAY. Home to 18.4 million people and counting, the city, formally known as Mumbai, is projected by 2015 to be the planet's second most populous metropolis, after Tokyo. Walk down its teeming streets, and you'll encounter crime lords and Bollywood stars, sprawling slums and Manhattan-priced condos, and jam-packed bars where DJs play the music of the Punjab, bhangra-a pulsating sound track familiar to club-goers in London and New York City. Bombay is where Wall Street gets equities analyzed, where a phone operator who calls herself Mary (but is really Meenakshi) sells Texans on two-week vacations that include the Taj-Mahal and cut rate heart surgery, will touch down in Bombay, since 40% of international flights to India land here, delivering thousands of new visitors every day.

India has the same problems that Africa has poor infrastructure, weak government, searing inequality, corruption and crime. India boasts more billionaires than China, Africa below the sub Saharan has only a few. 81% of India's population lives on $2 a day or less, compared with 47% of Chinese, according to the 2005 U.N. Population Reference Bureau Report. The class divide is starkest in cities like Bombay, where million0dollar apartments overlook million-population slums. For all its glitz, Bombay remains a temple of inefficiency.

But India does possess one indispensable asset, which has sustained its democracy and catapulted it to the cusp of global power: The ingenuity of its citizens. And nowhere is it in greater supply than in Bombay. "Because people have to make things work themselves", says Sanjay Bhandarkar, managing director of investment bank Rothschild's India. The rise of China has been the product of methodical state planning, but India's is all about private hustle, a trait that Americans can appreciate. Rakesh Jhunjhunwala, a billionaire trader in Bombay, says initiative represents Bombay's and India's advantage over the competitors. "It's people who make countries," he says. "not governments."

Since the Portuguese took possession of seven malarial Islands off the West Indian coast in 1534 and called them Good Bay. Now called

Bombay, has brimmed with entrepreneurs. Five centuries of migration have made Bombay the largest commercial center between Europe and the Far East.

Once you reach downtown Bombay you find a tropical British city of Victorian railway stations, Art Deco apartment blocks and Edwardian offices. Drive and purpose are the ingredients that make up the subcontinent's New York City atmosphere. "Pull anyone out of any part of India, and put them in Bombay", says Rothschild's Bhandarkar, "and he'll acquire that sense of drive and purpose". India's greatest industrialists, the Tatas, the Ambanis, and the Godrjs, all began in Bombay. The city's stock exchanges account for 92% of the country's total share turnover, and the nation's central bank and hundreds of brokerages and investors have set up their Indian headquarters there, including such global powerhouses as HSBC, JPMorgan Chase and Bank of America.

Bombay's port handles half of India's trade, and its southern business district is one of the centers of the global outsourcing boom. India's music industry and much of its media are based in Bombay, as is India's Hindi film industry, Bollywood. Such a concentration of business activity breeds a sophisticated; cosmopolitan outlook-hence Bombay has India's best hotels, bars, restaurants and nightclubs. And every day, according to the official census, hundreds move to the city to seek their fortune.

Ten ways India is changing the world:

1. India's GOP topped $800 billion in 2005. The economy has grown an average of 8% over the past 3 years, the fastest rate in the world.
2. India's internet-technology industry, which includes other outsourcing services, generated revenues of $36 billion in 2005, up 28% from 2004.
3. A surging stock market has boosted the number of Indian billionaires to 23, 10 of whom are new this year, compared with 8 in China. India's billionaires boast a combined net worth of $99 billion, an increase of 60% from the year before.
4. Since 1996, the number of Indian passengers of airlines has risen sixfold, to about 50 million travelers a year, and sales of motorcycles and passenger cars have doubled.
5. India's $1.5 billion film industry is the largest in the world, both in number of movies produced and in number of tickets sold. India makes close to 1,000 movies a year, five times Hollywood's output.

6. Tourism to India has risen about 20% over the past two years. Some 618,000 Americans flocked to India last year, making up nearly 16% of India's total visitors.
7. About 2 million people of Indian descent live in the U.S. The average household income of Indian Immigrants in the U.S. is the highest of any ethnic group.
8. Home to more than 1 billion people, India accounts for one-sixth of the world's population. In less than 50 years, it's expected to be the world's most populous nation.
9. India has more people living with HIV, an estimated 5.7 million, than any other country. This is a brewing crisis.
10. India lags behind China in GDP and foreign direct investment. But India is freer and growing faster, which may well give it the edge over the long haul.

These 10 ways India is changing the world comes from Time magazine article. Sources: World Bank, U.N., McKinsey & Co., and Price/ Waterhouse.

China, India & Africa's Future:

China and India are home to a third of the world's population. And they're undergoing social and economic revolutions that are capturing the best minds and money of Western business. The entrepreneurial forces driving China's and India's trajectories of development must be adopted my Africa below the Sub-Saharan, the Afro Asian Connection is vital to its survival.

According to Professor Tarun Khanna of Harvard Business School and author of Billions of Entrepreneurs, "today's economic projections suggest that in less than a generation China and India will become the largest and third-largest world economies, respectively and together they will account for nearly 40 percent of world trade".

African-Americans now have a tremendous opportunity and an obligation to participate, along with Asians, to invest. There's big money to be made by investing in small and risky businesses throughout Africa.

References

Why Africa Is Losing Race for Global Trade

BY CARL T. HALL

Chronicle Staff Writer

War in Somalia and the dismantling of apartheid in South Africa have focused new attention on the economic plight — and promise — of Africa.

Blessed with rich natural resources, but cursed by the legacy of colonialism, most of black Africa barely shows up on the map of global industry and trade. Living standards have dropped precipitously in recent years, squeezed by falling commodity prices and the crush of international debt.

By and large, African countries have not participated in the great burst of manufacturing trade that has swept through Asia and other parts of the world, said Elliot Berg, a consultant on Africa who is based near Washington, D.C. "There's no China — no Little Tigers."

In today's global economy, just about anything can be produced just about anywhere — for ultimate sale anywhere else. That has fostered a rise in trade and economic activity in many impoverished corners of Asia and Latin America. East Asia, paced by the extraordinary recent growth in China's economy, raised its GDP per capita by a phenomenal 7.2 percent last year.

The United States wants to bring Mexico into a regional zone of economic cooperation. Western Europe is struggling to integrate the former Eastern bloc countries. Japanese and Korean financiers are looking mainly in Asia for new places to invest.

Hardly anybody looks at Africa — at least until troubles explode in ways the world cannot ignore, as has happened in Angola and Somalia.

Sub-Saharan Africa as a whole appears to be withdrawing from an already minimal role in world trade. The most recent figures show that the region accounted for 2.2 percent of global trade in 1979, 1.3

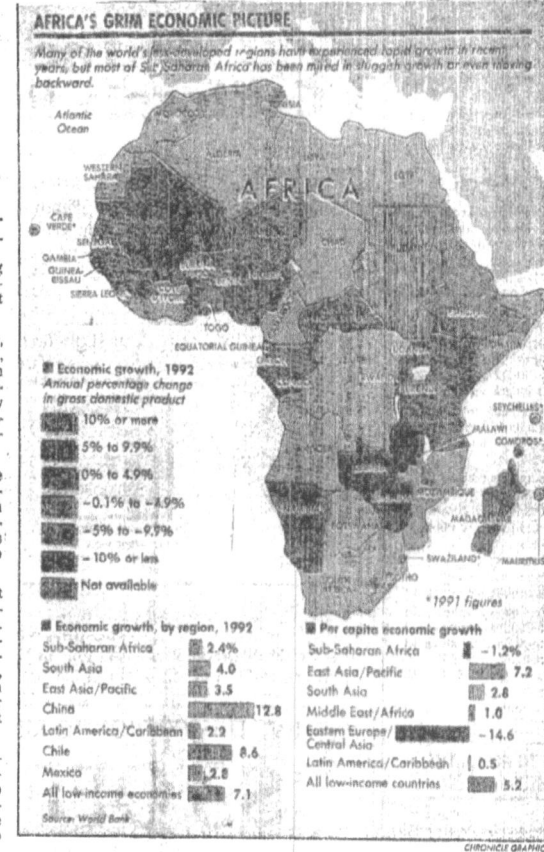

AFRICA'S GRIM ECONOMIC PICTURE

Many of the world's less-developed regions have experienced rapid growth in recent years, but most of Sub-Saharan Africa has been mired in sluggish growth or even moving backward.

Economic growth, 1992
Annual percentage change in gross domestic product

- 10% or more
- 5% to 9.9%
- 0% to 4.9%
- −0.1% to −4.9%
- −5% to −9.9%
- −10% or less
- Not available

*1991 figures

Economic growth, by region, 1992

Sub-Saharan Africa	2.4%
South Asia	4.0
East Asia/Pacific	3.5
China	12.8
Latin America/Caribbean	2.2
Chile	8.6
Mexico	2.8
All low-income economies	7.1

Source: World Bank

Per capita economic growth

Sub-Saharan Africa	−1.2%
East Asia/Pacific	7.2
South Asia	2.8
Middle East/Africa	1.0
Eastern Europe/Central Asia	−14.6
Latin America/Caribbean	0.5
All low-income countries	5.2

CHRONICLE GRAPHIC

percent in 1984 and just 1.1 percent in 1991.

Marina Ottaway, Africa specialist at the Washington-based Overseas Development Council, cited a long list of problems: lack of working transportation systems and infrastructure, poor health and education, bloated or corrupt government, ethnic strife and human-rights abuses by entrenched ruling elites.

Some blame policy blunders by the World Bank and International Monetary Fund, which in the early 1980s undertook an effort to promote what they called economic "structural reform" in the Third World. "The impact has been absolutely devastating on Africa, for the population generally and for women and children in

AFRICA: Page B7 Col. 2

51

AFRICA: Losing the Race for Global Trade

executive director of the Washington-based Development GAP, a private group often critical of World Bank policies.

Oxfam say the problem is that structural reforms — which typically include currency realignment, privatization and less involvement by government in setting prices — have not gone nearly far enough.

Nonetheless, there are some foreign firms. Western energy companies have been looking increasingly to Africa for crude-oil supplies, lured by the continent's estimated 80.4 million barrels in proven reserves — the third-largest cache in the world.

Much is riding on the outcome of longshot political and economic reforms under way throughout the continent — most notably the push for free elections and majority rule in South Africa. As South Africa sheds its status as international pariah, the nation's relatively advanced economy promises to serve as an important and badly needed anchor for the region.

With a free South Africa, "you could get a lot more healthy economic interchange" among the southern Africa nations and an increase in foreign investment, said Bronwen Manby, of Africa Watch, a New York-based human-rights organization. But she noted that nobody is expecting miracles. There are bound to be setbacks during what may prove to be a long transition period. Africa Watch estimates that reforms notwithstanding, more than 3,000 South Africans have been killed in political violence during the first nine months of this year.

While Africa's 52 independent nations are diverse in many ways, the economic statistics for most of black Africa — principally the 42 Sub-Saharan countries — paint a uniformly grim picture.

One of the best measures of liv-

years for the Sub-Sahara. Last year, per-capita GDP fell 1.2 percent.

Widespread Poverty

Oxfam, a British relief charity, estimates that without a substantial economic recovery, 300 million African people — half the continent's population — are destined to live in poverty, compared with 216 million now.

An estimated 6 million Africans are believed to be infected with HIV, the virus that causes AIDS, and a million Africans have died of the disease. Ten percent of Ugandans are believed to be infected.

Ishrat Husain, chief economist said that about 15 African countries — among them Ghana, Uganda, Kenya and Tanzania — have embarked on what he considers "a sustained path of economic reform" under World Bank tutelage. While changes have not been easy, many of these countries "have returned their economic declines and in some cases "are doing quite well," he said.

Ghana achieved a 5.1 percent increase in economic activity last year. Tanzania has been growing at about a 4 percent annual rate. Kenya has slowed after racking up four years of growth in the 4-percent-to-7-percent range.

But even in countries that have followed World Bank/IMF advice, the results have been "to put it mildly, disappointing," Ottaway said.

Beyond Africa's Control

While the debate goes on about what ought to be done about that, there is widespread agreement on one crucial point: Much of the trouble is beyond Africa's control.

The colonial period left almost all of Africa's 56 independent nations geared to producing just a few basic commodities — notably tin, copper and tea. African coun-

least until troubles explode in ways the world cannot ignore, as has happened in Angola and Somalia.

Sub-Saharan Africa as a whole appears to be withdrawing from an already minimal role in world trade. The most recent figures show that the region accounted for 2.2 percent of global trade in 1979, 1.3

1991.

Marina Ottaway, Africa specialist at the Washington-based Overseas Development Council, cited a long list of problems: lack of working transportation systems and infrastructure, poor health and education, bloated or corrupt government, ethnic strife and human-rights abuses by entrenched ruling elites.

World Bank and International Monetary Fund, which in the early 1980s undertook an effort to promote what they called economic "structural reform" in the Third World. "The impact has been absolutely devastating on Africa, for the population generally and for women and children in

AFRICA: Page B7 Col. 2

INTERACTION COUNCIL

Report on the Conclusions and Recommendations
by a High-level Group on

BRINGING AFRICA BACK TO THE MAINSTREAM OF THE INTERNATIONAL SYSTEM[1]

Chaired by
LORD CALLAGHAN OF CARDIFF

Cape Town, South Africa
21-23 January 1993

---

[1]   In addition to Lord Callaghan the following members of the InterAction Council participated in the meeting: Maria de Lourdes Pintasilgo (Portugal), Kenneth Kaunda (Zambia), Lopo Fortunato do Nascimento (Angola), Olusegun Obasanjo (Nigeria);
as well as the following high-level personalities
Alex Boraine (South Africa), Karen Brutenz (Russia), Pierre-Claver Damiba (Burkina Faso), Francis Deng (Sudan), Marion Graefin Doenhoff (Germany), Barend du Plessis (South Africa), Louis Emmerij (Netherlands), Adrian Hewitt (United Kingdom), Mostafa Khalil (Egypt), Colin Legum (United Kingdom), Daniel M. Lisulo (Zambia), Graca Machel (Mozambique), Robert McNamara (United States of America), Nthatho Motlana (South Africa), Olara Otunnu (Uganda), Ahmedou Ould Abdallah (Mauritania), Roy A. Pitchford (Zimbabwe), Ronald W. Roskens (United States of America), Fred Sai (Ghana), Tim Thahane (Lesotho), Makoto Watanabe (Japan) and as invited journalist Richard Steyn (South Africa).

PHOTO SPECIAL: SUMMER'S HOTTEST STARS

Newsweek

SPECIAL REPORT

China's Century

Actress
Ziyi Zhang,
the face of a
new China.

AFTER THE
HURRICANE

The Agony of
Africa

BusinessWeek

MAY 17, 1993   A McGRAW-HILL PUBLICATION $2.75

CHINA

THE
MAKING
OF AN
ECONOMIC
GIANT

SPECIAL REPORT

PAGE 54